Celebrity Snapper!

Taking the Ultimate Celebrity Photo

Susie Hodge

Capstone
press

Mankato, Minnesota

Fact Finders is published by Capstone Press,
a Capstone Publishers company.
151 Good Counsel Drive, P.O. Box 669,
Mankato, Minnesota 56002.
www.capstonepress.com

First published 2008
Copyright © 2008 A & C Black Publishers Limited

Produced for A & C Black by

Monkey Puzzle Media Ltd
The Rectory, Eyke, Woodbridge,
Suffolk IP12 2QW, UK

Library of Congress Cataloging-in-Publication Data

Hodge, Susie, 1960-
   Celebrity snapper : taking the ultimate celebrity photo /
by Susie Hodge.
     p. cm. -- (Fact finders. Extreme!)
Includes bibliographical references and index.
ummary: "Presents the science behind celebrity
   photography including the history, techniques, and tools
   of the paparazzi"--Provided by publisher.
   ISBN-13: 978-1-4296-3119-8 (hardcover : alk. paper)
   ISBN-10: 1-4296-3119-8 (hardcover : alk. paper)
   ISBN-13: 978-1-4296-3139-6 (softcover : alk. paper)
   ISBN-10: 1-4296-3139-2 (softcover : alk. paper)
1. Celebrities--Portraits--Juvenile literature. 2. Portrait
photography--Juvenile literature. 3. Paparazzi--Juvenile
literature. I. Title. II. Series.

TR681.F3H63 2009
779'.2092--dc22

2008025663

Editor: Polly Goodman
Design: Mayer Media Ltd
Picture research: Lynda Lines
Series consultant: Jane Turner

This book is produced using paper that is made from
wood grown in managed, sustainable forests. It is natural,
renewable, and recyclable. The logging and manufacturing
processes conform to the environmental regulations of
the country of origin.

Printed in the United States of America

Picture acknowledgements
Corbis pp. 5 (Patrick Giardino), 6 (Sunset Boulevard), 7
(Hulton-Deutsch Collection), 11 (David Pu'u), 15 (Mario
Anzuoni/Reuters), 18 (Dusko Despotovic), 19 (David
Koskas), 20 (Lucas Jackson/Reuters), 22 (Alessia
Pierdomenico/Reuters); Getty Images pp. 1, 4, 9 (Ryan
McVay), 13, 14, 24 (James Devaney), 25, 28; iStockphoto
pp. 8 top, 8 bottom left; MPM Images pp. 8 bottom left,
10; Reuters p. 23 (Kiyoshi Ota); Rex Features pp. 12
(Julian Makey), 16 (Dave Lewis), 17 (Mr. JCY); Richard
Young Photography pp. 26, 27; Topfoto pp. 21 both
(National Pictures), 29 (PA).

The front cover shows a paparrazzi photographer with
a "Map to the Stars' Homes" in Los Angeles, California
(Corbis/Richard Ransier).

Every effort has been made to contact copyright holders
of material reproduced in this book. Any omissions will be
rectified in subsequent printings if notice is given to the
publishers.

CONTENTS

Abbreviations m stands for meters • **ft** stands for feet • **in** stands for inches •
km stands for kilometers

Who are the paparazzi?

People love finding out what celebrities are up to. That creates lots of work for extreme photographers, called the paparazzi.

Paparazzi are photographers who are constantly on the hunt for celebrities and public figures. The best paparazzi photos can be sold for hundreds of thousands of dollars. Those prices mean it's very competitive, and paparazzi take more and more risks to get a front-page picture.

The actress Portia de Rossi arrives at the Oscars in Hollywood in February 2007. Most celebrities like being photographed when they're looking their best!

La Dolce Vita

The word *paparazzi* comes from a film called *La Dolce Vita*, which was made in 1960. In it, there was a celebrity photographer called Paparazzo.

celebrities people who are famous

How do paparazzi get their shots?

What are the tricks of the trade?

What kind of equipment do they use?

paparazzi photographers who take photographs of celebrities

The first paparazzi

When **portrait photography** was invented in the 1840s, people rushed to have their photos taken. Many people believed that, unlike painting, photography was a science that revealed the truth.

Photographers knew, however, that they could bend the truth in the way they took photos. Early photographs of famous figures were carefully planned, just like paintings. It wasn't until the mid-20th century that photographers snapped pictures without setting them up first.

From the 1840s to the 1950s, most celebrity portrait photos were dramatic and carefully planned. They were often **retouched** *by hand with paint after the photo was printed, to please the celebrity.*

Flattering photos

To make a celebrity look softer in a photo, sometimes petroleum jelly was smeared on the camera lens. To make the photo sharp and dramatic, a light was reflected off a shiny surface to light up the face.

portrait photography   the photography of individual people

For early photos, any movement would ruin the picture. No wonder people rarely smiled for the photographer!

Metal clamp held the head still.

Person had to sit rigidly still for up to 30 minutes.

retouched when a photograph is improved or changed by adding details or removing faults

Lights, camera, action!

Just think. Every time you see something, your eyes are taking a picture, like a camera constantly at work.

Cameras work just like human eyes. They both have a **lens** that focuses light through a small hole. Light travels from the subject of a photo through the camera lens and is recorded as an image on a **sensor**. This is the same as light traveling through the eye to the **retina**.

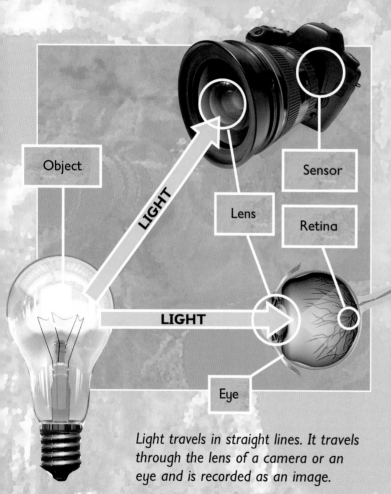

Object

LIGHT

Lens

Sensor

Retina

LIGHT

Eye

Light travels in straight lines. It travels through the lens of a camera or an eye and is recorded as an image.

Taking a photo

To take a photo, you press a button on the camera to open the **shutter**, which lets light into the camera. The amount of time the shutter is open controls how much light reaches the sensor.

lens   part of a camera or eye that focuses an image

Photographers take photos of a model on a catwalk.

Stage lights point at the catwalk.

Light bounces off the celebrity and travels to camera.

Light is recorded as an image in the camera.

LIGHT

LIGHT

Click!

Click!

Click!

sensor part of a camera that records an image   **retina** lining on the back of the eye

Color and light

You might think that there are hundreds of different colors, but all the different shades that you see are blended together out of just seven basic colors—the colors that make up white light.

The seven colors in light were first identified in 1666. A scientist named Isaac Newton discovered that if you shine light through a **prism**, it separates out into the colors of the **spectrum**: red, orange, yellow, green, blue, indigo, and violet.

You can see the colored dots of ink in this close-up of a color print.

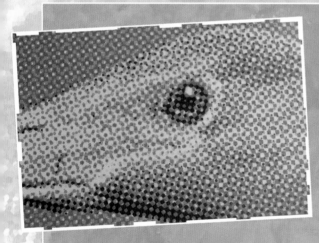

Color printing

Although light is made up of seven colors, photos are printed using just three colored inks—cyan, magenta, yellow—plus black. Tiny dots of ink are used rather than solid blocks of color. The amount of dots that are used create different shades.

prism   a glass pyramid that splits white light into the colors of the spectrum

Tiny droplets of water vapor in the air work like prisms. They can separate light into the colors of the spectrum, creating a rainbow.

RED
ORANGE
YELLOW
GREEN
BLUE
INDIGO
VIOLET

White light contains all the colors of the spectrum blended together.

In a rainbow, the colors of white light are separated out.

spectrum   the seven colors in a rainbow, which make up white light

Flash power

Much of the paparazzi's work takes place at night, as celebrities leave nightclubs, restaurants, or hotels. Fortunately for the paps, there are ways of taking photos even on the darkest of nights.

Unlike our eyes, cameras don't automatically adjust to changes in light. At night, there is not enough natural light to get a clear picture, so photographers make their own light using **flash**. Electronic flashes send out a short burst of bright light, which lights up the **subject** for a moment.

Camera flashes make the subject bright but the background dark, so the subject shows up more.

flash a small, bright lamp that gives a quick burst of light to take a photograph

Fast!
Light travels at about 186,000 miles (300,000 km) per second.

Flash!
Camera flash travels to the face in a split second.

LIGHT

LIGHT

Bounce!
Light bounces off the face and travels back to the camera.

Singer Jay Kay is caught in a paparazzo's camera flash as he is bundled into a car by security men.

subject in photography, the object that is being photographed

13

Exposed!

When paparazzi want to take photos at night without being spotted or given away by their flash, they increase the exposure on their cameras.

The exposure is the amount of light that gets into a camera. It is controlled by the **aperture** and shutter speed. The aperture is how wide the shutter opens. In dim light, it can be made wider to let in more light. The shutter speed is the length of time the shutter stays open. In dim light, it is made slower to let in more light.

In dark conditions, the aperture is wide and the shutter speed is slow. The shutter should be kept open for between three and 30 seconds.

The photographer increased the exposure for this photograph to let enough light into the camera.

aperture   the opening in a lens that lets light into a camera

In lighter conditions, the aperture can be narrower and the shutter speed faster—between one and three seconds.

exposure   the amount of light that can get into a camera

The hunt and chase

Paparazzi go to great lengths to find celebrities. They work like private detectives, paying contacts to let them know when their targets might appear. Then they use extreme tactics to get to them.

Some paparazzi perch in trees or on rooftops. Others rent helicopters or boats to photograph private events. Some even disguise themselves as waiters, policemen, or cleaners to catch celebrities unaware.

Living dangerously—a paparazzo hangs out of a helicopter with his camera hundreds of feet up in the air.

Dangerous tactics

Snatching photos of people who don't want to be photographed started in the 1930s. It might look exciting, but paparazzi tactics can be deadly dangerous. Princess Diana died following a high-speed chase involving the paparazzi in 1997.

contacts   people who have useful connections to celebrities or events

These two photographers climbed up 15 ft (5 m) of scaffolding to take photos of a celebrity in a hotel room across the street.

Celebrity in hotel room across the street.

Paparazzi hide in scaffolding. They'll wait there for hours, if necessary, just for one shot.

They cut holes in the netting to get a clear shot.

Long-distance photos

When celebrities are relaxing on remote beaches or distant private yachts, it is sometimes impossible to get up close. So the paparazzi have to take photos from a distance.

To take photos of celebrities from far away, the paparazzi use cameras with **telephoto** and **zoom lenses**. These lenses can take pictures of objects up to 30 miles (48 kilometers) away. The celebrities are often completely unaware that they are being photographed.

When celebrities don't notice the photographer, they are more likely to act naturally.

No privacy

Many celebrities get very angry when they are photographed secretly because they feel they don't have any privacy. In 2005, Angelina Jolie was upset when she was shown photos of herself on vacation in Africa with Brad Pitt. The pictures had been taken from about 6 miles (10 kilometers) away.

telephoto lenses   lenses on a camera that make an image appear larger

Telephoto lens

Celebrity on beach

Paparazzi hide behind rocks.

zoom lenses lenses on a camera that make an image larger or smaller

Zooming in

Photographers use a variety of zoom and telephoto lenses at a top fashion show in New York City.

So how do telephoto and zoom lenses work? Both lenses can **magnify** everything, making the subject seem bigger.

A telephoto lens is a long lens that makes distant objects look bigger. This creates a photo that is similar to moving closer to the object. A zoom lens can make the subject bigger or smaller.

magnify to make larger

Telephoto lenses make distant objects appear **bigger.**

Some lenses make the pictures sharper.

Micro-cameras

You hear a click that sounds just like a camera, but there's no camera in sight ... you've probably been snapped by a micro-camera!

New technology has developed cameras so tiny that they now fit inside cell phones, portable media players, and even tie clips and pens. This means there are even more ways of taking celebrity snaps, and if you're in the right place at the right time, you could become a celebrity snapper, too!

A video camera is hidden in this pen!

Handkerchief snaps

In the mid-20th century, photographer Henri Cartier-Bresson sometimes wrapped a large handkerchief around his camera and would pretend to blow his nose while he took photos.

Video camera

Digital camera

Phone camera

Fans use all sorts of cameras to take photos of their favorite celebrities.

23

Red-carpet photography

At film premieres, award ceremonies, and celebrity parties, a different type of photographer snaps away at the side of the red carpet—these are event photographers, not paparazzi—and their job is quite different.

Celebrities know they will be captured on camera at events, and often the photos will help to **promote** a new book, song, or film. The celebrities usually turn up looking good and work with the photographers to make the best photos possible.

Some celebrities, like Paris Hilton, encourage photographers' attention. But if celebrities are photographed too often, their pictures become less valuable.

promote   to encourage the sale of something

On the red carpet, photographers compete with each other to get the best shots.

Photographers ask celebrities to stand in the spot with the best light.

Snap!

Click!

Celebrities often **pose** for the photographers to make the photo more interesting.

pose in photography, to take a special position or expression for a photograph

Before and after

In magazines and advertisements, people often look perfect. Many photos of celebrities or models are retouched before they are printed.

Before ...

There are many tricks that can be used on a photo to achieve the perfect look. Computer programs can smooth skin, lighten shadows under the eyes, and remove blemishes and wrinkles. Teeth can be straightened, hair color changed, eyebrows raised, and eye shapes altered.

Photo editing

Photographers often adjust, or **edit** their photos using computer programs before sending them to magazines. They can make the subject look more focused and make images sharper. This is called photo editing.

edit   to prepare something for printing

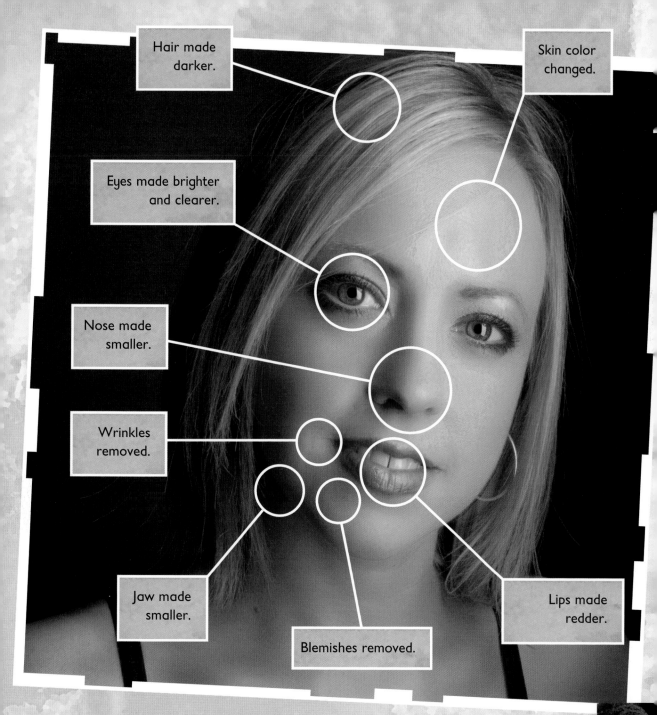

Hair made darker.

Skin color changed.

Eyes made brighter and clearer.

Nose made smaller.

Wrinkles removed.

Jaw made smaller.

Blemishes removed.

Lips made redder.

... and after. Most models don't look as good in real life as they do in magazines!

The need for speed

How do you take a photo of a sports celebrity whizzing past you at over 100 miles (160 kilometers) per hour?

At this racetrack pit stop, the fast action has been caught on camera and made to look blurred and distorted.

Photographers have two main ways of taking fast-action photos. They either "freeze" the action, making the subject sharp but leaving the background a blur, or they make the movement look blurred.

- For sharp action shots, photographers use fast shutter speeds.
- For blurred action shots, photographers use slower shutter speeds.

focus to point the lens of a camera at the subject and adjust the lens to get a clear picture

Capturing speed

To catch fast-moving subjects:
- **Focus** on your target.
- Stand in the best position.
- **Pan** ahead of the subject with your camera.
- Take several shots quickly.

Blurry background

Crystal-clear
subject

When photographers pan (move) their cameras to keep up with a moving subject, the subject appears to stay in place while other features stretch into streaks. This shows movement really well.

pan to move the camera while taking the photo

Glossary

aperture the opening in a lens that lets light into a camera

celebrities people who are famous

contacts people who have useful connections to celebrities or events

edit to prepare something for printing

exposure the amount of light that can get into a camera

flash a small, bright lamp that gives a quick burst of light to take a photograph

focus to point the lens of a camera at the subject and adjust the lens to get a clear picture

lens part of a camera or eye that focuses an image

magnify to make larger

pan to move the camera while taking the photo

paparazzi (singular: paparazzo) photographers who take photographs of celebrities

portrait photography the photography of individual people

pose in photography, to take a special position or expression for a photograph

prism a glass pyramid that splits white light into the colors of the spectrum

promote to encourage the sale of something

retina lining on the back of the eye

retouched when a photograph is improved or changed by adding details or removing faults

sensor part of a camera that records an image

shutter part of a camera that opens and closes to let in light

spectrum the seven colors in a rainbow, which make up white light

subject in photography, the object that is being photographed

telephoto lenses lenses on a camera that make an image appear larger

zoom lenses lenses on a camera that make an image larger or smaller

Further information

Books

Digital Photo Madness!: 50 Weird and Wacky Things to Do with Your Digital Camera by Thom Gaines (Lark Books, 2006)

Essential Science: Light and Seeing by Peter Riley (Watts, 2006)
Essential facts about light and sight with experiments.

How Does Science Work? Light by Carol Ballard (Hodder Wayland, 2006)
The science of light explained in clear and simple text.

The Kids' Guide to Digital Photography: How to Shoot, Save, Play With and Print Your Digital Photos by Jenni Bidner (Lark Books, 2004)

Paparazzi by Peter Howe (Artisan, 2005)
A big glossy book with photographs and stories by paparazzi.

Science Answers: Light by Chris Cooper (Heinemann, 2003)
Aspects of the science of light linked to everyday examples, including experiments.

Science in Your Life, Light: Look Out! by Wendy Sadler (Raintree, 2005)
An introduction to the science of light applied to everyday life.

Science Investigations: Light by John Gorman (Hodder Wayland, 2006)
A question-and-answer approach to the science of light.

Voyage of a Light Beam: Light Energy by Andrew Solway (Raintree, 2005)
An introduction to the science of light.

Web sites

FactHound offers a safe, fun way to find Internet sites related to this book. All of the sites on FactHound have been researched by our staff. Visit *www.facthound.com* for age-appropriate sites. You may browse subjects by clicking on letters, or by clicking on pictures and words.
FactHound will fetch the best sites for you!

Index